Rev. Wally Johnston 26-21

A LAYMAN'S GUIDE TO SANCTIFICATION

A LAYMAN'S GUIDE TO SANCTIFICATION

by

H. Ray Dunning, Ph.D.

BEACON HILL PRESS OF KANSAS CITY
KANSAS CITY, MISSOURI

ISBN: 083-411-3872

Printed in the
United States of America

Cover Design: Crandall Vail

Permission to quote from the following versions of Scripture is acknowledged with appreciation:

The Holy Bible, New International Version (NIV), copyright © 1973, 1978, 1984 by the International Bible Society. Used by permission of Zondervan Bible Publishers. Unless otherwise indicated, all Scripture quotations are from this version.

The *Revised Standard Version of the Bible* (RSV), copyrighted 1946, 1952, © 1971, 1973.

KJV – King James Version

10 9 8 7 6 5 4 3 2 1

CONTENTS

Foreword

Like learning to live with a limp, many fine folk among our holiness ranks have quietly given up on ever finding whatever it is that certain people have called the deeper life, entire sanctification, or Christian perfection, and they have settled for a second-class spiritual existence. Many of these folk have tried all the formulas for finding sanctifying grace only to come away empty, discouraged, or even tormented. Some have nearly experienced destabilizing nervous breakdowns trying to struggle into the experience they have heard described as the norm. In confusion and disappointment they have withdrawn in a sort of spiritual lack of self-esteem, figuring that there must be something wrong with them. They therefore settle for a permanent second-class citizenship in the kingdom of God. They do all right until the sermon or the conversation turns to entire sanctification. At that point they appear nervous, tense, or troubled like someone still trying to overcome an old grief. If you get within a heartbeat of them, you discover an inner sadness that has replaced hope for full salvation.

Another group of uneasy pilgrims among us is made up of those who have been rushed into a premature profession of sanctifying grace. They testified "by faith" to an experience they thought they were supposed to have and, wanting to do what God and the church expected, they "named it and claimed it." But, predictably, what they have experienced in their inmost heart is far short of the promises and sales pitches they heard in behalf of the holy life. Some then trivialize a great blessing, seeming to ask, "Is that all there is?" Some in this category come to regard the testimony (which they reluctantly but not joyfully give) as a sort of union card required by our fellowship.

These two groups have doggedly stuck with us, and we have yet another chance to introduce them to the comforts and joys of the sanctified life. Still another group, particularly among the young, have not been nearly so patient with us. When a gap appeared between what was proclaimed and promised and what was observed and experienced they quickly pitched the whole idea over and went to other churches, or in too many cases dropped out of the Christian fellowship altogether.

Melvin Dieter (a leading historian of the holiness movement) says that every generation in the holiness movement will look at its heritage as if it were an estate sale. At such an event all the belongings of a house or a family are placed on display in the unoccupied rooms, the veranda, and the lawn. Among the items up for bid are priceless family heirlooms, valuable works of art, useful tools—and lots of junk. The task of each generation is to tell the difference between the parts of the heritage that have timeless value and the parts of the heritage that are just "stuff." The younger, "in a hurry" generation may label it all "useless" and look for meaning elsewhere.

This book speaks particularly to the members of these three groups: those who have quietly accepted a second-class Christian walk, those who were rushed into claiming an experience of grace for which God had not yet had time to prepare them, and those who, noticing a gap between what was promised and preached and what was observed and experienced, are tempted to throw it all out.

The persons who inhabit these categories are not really to blame. They have heard many conflicting sermons, lessons, and testimonies about sanctification. Many uncertain trumpets have been blown. The teaching and preaching of entire sanctification has become in many areas a whirligig of abstractions or a quagmire of theological jargon. This confusing state of affairs did not come about because anyone was trying to be bad. It has, nevertheless, left the very ones to whom the "grand depositum" of sanctification has been entrusted among those who give the weakest witness to its reality.

A Look at the Past with Understanding

A hundred years ago our spiritual ancestors who led the American holiness movement saw the world they inherited crash in pieces at their feet.

What they had always believed about the Bible crumbled before the onslaught of European biblical criticism.

What they had always believed about their nation had just a generation before been shattered by the Civil War.

What they had always believed about the Christian faith withered before the attacks of what was then called "theological modernism."

What our spiritual ancestors had always believed about the origin and destiny of humankind was washed away like a sand castle at high tide in the eyes of many when Charles Darwin popularized and seemed to legitimize evolution.

What they had always believed about the nature of truth, reality, and value was punctured by the new pragmatic philosophy of the father of progressive education, John Dewey. Dewey, just after the turn of the century, surveyed the wreckage of the way the world had been and philosophized that perhaps there were after all no absolutes. Truth, right, and reality are whatever works, he declared.

And even as those early Nazarenes were gathering at Pilot Point, Tex., the thought of Sigmund Freud was festering in Europe and would soon challenge second generation Nazarenes about what they had always been taught about who and what they were as human beings. In popular thought man would become *id, ego,* and *superego* rather than *body, soul,* and *spirit*. The way was already paved for this by 1900 by men such as George Albert Coe, who had already nearly reduced Protestant Christian education to mental hygiene.

From the ruins of this multiple paradigm shift there

arose a breed of men and women who were not ready to give in to the popular trends of the day. They believed in traditional Christianity, the Bible, social justice, and holiness of heart and life. They were passionate and compassionate, conservative and tough, innovative and courageous, energetic and shrewd. They believed that what persons and nations needed was the doctrine and experience of entire sanctification. Like John Wesley they believed that sanctifying grace was God's cure for the private and corporate ills of the race.

This group spread revival, organized churches, established orphanages, and planted holiness colleges all over the landscape. They proclaimed timeless truths. They did a lot of things gloriously right.

They had, predictably, a natural built-in resistance to intellectuals. After all, it was the intellectuals – the scientists, theologians, philosophers, and scholars who could read Greek and Hebrew Bibles – who had destroyed the world they had inherited from their parents.

In an almost instinctive survival move they, more or less, cut themselves off from the biblical scholarship, the theological reflection, and the philosophical hypothesizing then taking place. Avoiding such things it is not surprising that the good people of this movement came early to rely heavily on testimony and religious experience. They developed a way of being that was long on personal experience and short on in-depth understanding of the Scriptures and open-minded theological reflection. Such an imbalance was almost bound to appear.

Avoiding intellectualism and relying heavily upon testimony and experience produced a phenomenon of all but codifying the experiences of the influential and gifted people. As they powerfully testified about how God broke through to them in sanctifying grace, the methods themselves became the rule and practice of many followers.

The movement became largely internally sufficient, with no need for outside counsel. As the movement gained strength and momentum it became more and more self-validating. In time it all but cut itself off even from its own roots in Wesleyanism. If you question ministers, as I have, who received their training in so-called Wesleyan colleges and seminaries within the holiness movement during the '40s, '50s, and '60s you will find that it was not at all unusual for a theological student to go through four years of college and three years of seminary without being required to read one page of Wesley's writings.

A Look at the Future with Hope

Since our courageous founding fathers and mothers first proclaimed "Holiness unto the Lord," at least two more cultural upheavals have affected the way North Americans think and make meaning. The theological clothes handed down from our grandfathers and grandmothers do not fit as comfortably as they once did. This is especially true for those who have come into our church without a background in the Church of the Nazarene or one of her sister holiness denominations.

The task of translating the tradition to each new generations in terms of the way they have learned to make meaning has not gone well in many quarters. It has not been helped by the idea that the way to preserve the heritage is to say everything the very same way that those beloved agrarian forefathers of ours stated them.

The limited success we have had in transferring the key principles of the Wesleyan/holiness tradition has left us with a lot of bafflement, pain, and no small degree of identity confusion. The times call for gentle and wise teachers who love the tradition and desire to put our people back in touch with the richest part of our heritage.

Ray Dunning is just such a teacher. He is a man who can effectively serve as God's usher for those who hunger and thirst after righteousness. The literature on spiritual guidance tells us that a spiritual guide should be loving and learned, characterized by tender respect, holiness, patience, theological competence, the gift of discernment, frankness, honesty, and availability to the Holy Spirit. On all these counts Dr. Dunning measures up. He is eminently qualified to patiently and gently teach us again the treasures of our tradition of scriptural holiness.

In this little book Dr. Dunning invites us into his living room for some quiet talks on holiness. You will especially appreciate his calling us back to the biblical meanings and descriptions of the holy life. Also, he helps us recognize the value in prizing and owning our indebtedness to John Wesley. His biblical definition of Christian perfection is insightful. The connection between sanctification and love is lucidly described. Holiness as the restoration of the image of God is explored in harmony with the teachings of John Wesley. The joy and comfort of the pursuit of perfection is treated in a very helpful way.

I suggest this book be read quickly for an overview and then read a second time devotionally as a part of one's private worship. Most important—try to come to this book with an open mind. Come to it as though you were hearing about sanctification for the first time.

—WESLEY D. TRACY

A Note to the Reader

The title of this essay needs some clarification. The term *layman* should not be understood as a class of persons who are not clergy. That is one appropriate use of the term, but basically it refers to any person in relation to any field in which he or she is not trained in the technical aspects of that field. For instance, I am interested in science, but I am a layman when it comes to being conversant with the technology, scientific jargon, and many theories that are items of daily conversation among trained scientists. Thus I enjoy reading nontechnical works in various aspects of science, but when it becomes very technical, I have to throw in the towel. In like fashion many people – even clergy – are not trained theologians and thus are laymen (or laypersons). There is nothing derogatory in this language and certainly no one should ever refer to himself as "just a layman," especially in the church. But it is true that certain persons in the church have spent their lives studying and training in the technical aspects of theology. Unfortunately, too often these theologians talk in specialized language that is over the heads of the nontechnician. Equally unfortunate is the fact that many laymen in theology present themselves as experts and sometimes even challenge the conclusions of the formally trained theologian. They would never think of doing so in most other fields.

It is the purpose of this essay to avoid as much insider talk as possible so that any reader may have an informed introduction to this great theme.

Preface

This little book is the result of two factors. The first was the earnest questioning of laypersons in places where I have preached. Sensitive, intelligent, and loyal churchmen often expressed serious problems with the stereotyped formulas they had heard in attempts to explain what sanctification is all about. They sincerely desired to hear more adequate answers to their questions. Most seemed satisfied with the approach embodied in this essay. It made sense to them because it had the possibility of practical application to daily living. The truth is that theology must be livable or it has no credibility in the marketplace of the church.

The second factor was the expression of a need for such a work by Rev. Paul Neal at the NPH sales representatives meeting in preparation for the 1990 District Assembly season. All the representatives concurred with the need for something on sanctification to make available to their constituency who, they said, were always asking for a simple treatment of the subject. As Paul and I talked about the need, a fire kindled in my heart to do something about it.

It would be asking too much to expect that these simple words will answer everyone's questions. But the basic issues that arise in most discussions are addressed with the attempt to present an informed response. Every effort has been made to avoid as much technical jargon as possible, but some is unavoidable if the treatment is to be adequate. However, care has been taken to explain all such language and concepts.

The reader should be aware that each part of this essay supplements the other parts. Thus it is more appropriate to study the material herein and cross-reference it for better understanding.

While this book is designed as a nontechnical treatment, there are several endnote references. One purpose of this is to provide resources for any who would desire to pursue further some of the matters addressed. It also seeks to avoid the charge of using others' material without giving credit. The Bibliography at the close provides additional resources for any who would like to read more deeply into the theme of sanctification.

Introduction: Who Is Confused About Sanctification?

Sanctification is a big theological word. Some people avoid words more than two syllables long – especially theological words. But the real problem with this word is not the number of syllables it contains (five, I think) but the fact that there is such a bewildering variety of views as to what it means. The result is that many people are frustrated and confused and consequently decide to simply keep quiet about the whole thing. When you add the word *entire* to *sanctification,* the confusion multiplies.

Why is there such a difference of opinion among Christians on this topic? Even more perplexing, why is there such a diversity of views among persons who are part of the "holiness movement"? Let me suggest a couple of reasons:

First, many interpreters explain what "happens" in an experience called *entire sanctification* in terms of their personal experience. In preparation for writing this essay I read several books and articles by people who professed to be providing a simple explanation of this doctrine and experience. Most of what I found was a description of their own ideal personality traits. What they were doing was seeking to universalize their own experiences, that is, make them the standard for all persons. In one particular instance, I knew the author quite well and clearly recognized my friend's personality type in the list of results of entire sanctification he described.

But there is an endless variety of personalities, and if every one became the standard for every other person, the result would be chaos. The real problem comes with strong, dominant personalities who "steamroll" others with differing temperaments. The unfortunate result is that people either submit to the pressure and become clones or else flee an uncomfortable situation. This may account for many former "holiness people" who are in nonholiness denominations. What is the answer to this "blooming, buzzing confusion"? The answer is to return to Scripture as a benchmark and allow biblical concepts to determine our doctrine and experience.

Another reason for the widespread confusion in the contemporary holiness churches is that the term *sanctification* is used in several different ways, both in theology and in the Bible. We don't seem to have much trouble with everyday language being used with multiple meanings, but we react negatively when religious language functions in the same complex way. For example, no one raises an eyebrow when we use the word *strike*. We simply want to know what "game" is being played. Are we bowling, playing baseball, fishing, or prizefighting? Why not take the same approach to the language of religion and ask, What does this term mean in this context?

This approach has implications for where we go to find what words mean. First, we should not turn to Webster's dictionary as the source of our theology. It records how words are used in general at the present time. Perhaps we could use a Bible dictionary or a dictionary of theology, but the best way is to trace the concept through Scripture, allowing how the writers use the term to dictate what it means. Furthermore, we should not be restricted to the words *sanctify, sanctification,* and *holiness.* The truth of sanctification extends well beyond those passages of Scripture that use the specific terms. A whole collection of terms and concepts relate to the larger significance of sanctification. Examples are *perfection, the image of God, love, discipleship,* and many others less directly. We will be exploring the major terms in this essay.

Furthermore, one cannot point to specific texts that say precisely what we are accustomed to hearing from popular teachers and preachers about the doctrine of sanctification. For instance, we look in vain to the preaching of Jesus for the standard terminology and structures we are accustomed to associating with "holiness" preaching and teaching. Why is that?

Two reasons may be suggested. First, theology is the attempt to state the biblical message in logical form using contemporary language. In doing so it gives specific structures to Christian beliefs. In thus formulating biblical teaching in doctrinal propositions it often uses language and formulas that go beyond the exact wording of Scripture. We become so familiar with these that we are often shocked to realize that they are the product of theologians at work instead of a repetition of biblical terms and phrases. Sometimes we become so attached to these particular formulations that we resist new and different ways of attempting to recover the truth found in Scripture. This inflexibility and lack of openness to new ways of understanding has been called a "hardening of the categories."

We have to admit that this puts us at a disadvantage with those who insist that every religious claim must be supported by a literal statement of Scripture. But we have no other choice since the Bible does not contain many formal theological statements, and most Christian beliefs cannot be supported in this simplistic way.

There is also a second reason it is difficult to cite proof texts for some doctrinal formulations, especially concerning holiness in Christian experience. Our understanding is not drawn from specific texts as much as from a holistic interpretation of biblical theology. As W. T. Purkiser said: "The doctrine of Christian holiness is based upon the total thrust of Scriptures. It is not merely a thread or line of truth running through the Word of God. It is rather a network of teaching which is an essential part of the fabric of the whole."[1]

This suggests that we have to take a more wide-ranging approach to Scripture. Rather than citing proof texts for the doctrine of sanctification, we must appeal to the larger structure of biblical theology.[2] With this in mind we want to trace some of these major themes about sanctification through the larger teaching of Scripture as well as survey a variety of topics that make up the collage of biblical sanctification.

PART I

WHAT IN THE *BIBLE* IS SANCTIFICATION?

1

Sanctification in the Old Testament

The Book of Leviticus contains the most extended discussions of holiness (the basic word) and sanctification (the act or process by which something or someone is made holy) found in the Old Testament. In fact, holiness is the key concept in this book. But most of us don't read Leviticus because we feel that all those discussions about dietary laws, rituals of purification, and so on, have been done away in Jesus Christ. As a result, we don't pay much attention to the best source for understanding the idea of holiness.

"Be ye holy for I am holy" is the motto of Leviticus. It is repeated four times (11:44-45; 19:2; 20:26). This motto suggests three important truths to us:

1. God alone is holy in himself. Because it is His holiness that defines who God is, and definitions limit what is being defined, and God cannot be limited, no effort is made to define what it means. The nearest to a suggestion as to its meaning is the teaching that God's name is profaned by idolatry, swearing falsely, and other sins (18:21; 19:17; 21:6; 22:2). This means that He demonstrates His holiness in judging sin (see 10:3; Num. 20:13). "Holiness is intrinsic to God's character."[3]

2. Holiness in human beings (or things) is present only when in relation to God. That is, no finite person or object has any inherent holiness. The holiness of things and persons is derived and dependent. This derived holiness is present only so long as the person or thing is in right relation to God.

3. Holiness in human beings is understood to be "godlikeness." But there is a problem. If God's holiness is not defined in any positive sense (see No. 1), how can one know what it means to "be holy as God is holy"? Here is where we get the most help from Leviticus. The strange thing is that this motto is set right in the middle of a lengthy discussion about clean and unclean foods and in other settings concerned with matters that seem to us to be irrelevant to Christian faith. But perhaps it is precisely this setting that will throw some light on the meaning of holiness in human experience.

Animals that are unclean are those that have characteristics from two realms. For example, a catfish swims in the water but does not have scales, which seem appropriate to a fish. The best suggestion is that holiness requires that different classes of things not be confused. The same thing seems to be implied in the command that mixed materials are not to be used. Mixed seeds are not to be sown, mixed cloth is not to be used in a garment. Furthermore, persons who are deformed are forbidden to serve in the tabernacle. All this suggests that holiness in human experience implies wholeness, integrity, and normality. Some commentators say that the distinction between clean and unclean animals was to remind Israel that God had distinguished them from all other nations on earth to be His own possession, that is, it implies that holiness implies separation *from* the unclean and *to* the holy God.

These insights are very helpful in seeing that holiness is not an abnormal condition, something that warps and/or twists one's personality. On the contrary, this truth suggests that the holy life results in our being more human and not less human.

In the Old Testament one is made holy, or sanctified by certain rituals, such as sprinkling of blood or other acts of purification. This could degenerate into mere ritualism, that is, participating in the ritual without there being any ethical change. The ritual could become an empty ceremony – and this frequently happened to the Israelites. This became one of the major sources of tension between priest and prophet. Note the dramatic confrontation between Amos and Amaziah as recorded in Amos 7:10-15. The prophets repeatedly condemn the practice of going through the acts of religion but not living according to the covenant laws.

Because of this there arose the hope that in time to come God would make provision for a real change of the human heart so that instead of sanctification being an external activity, it would be an inward, ethical transformation. Jeremiah speaks about a new covenant in which God would write the law on the heart (Jer. 31:31 ff.), and Ezekiel hears the Lord promise, "I will give you a new heart and put a new spirit in you; I will remove from you your heart of stone and give you a heart of flesh. And I will put my Spirit in you and move you to follow my decrees and be careful to keep my laws" (Ezek. 36:26-27).

After the close of the Old Testament, the rabbis continued to express this hope of inward sanctification. They believed that when the new age of the Spirit dawned, "The evil impulse would be taken out of Israel's heart . . . and the Spirit, as a power for moral renewal would rest upon her."[4]

SPIRITUAL FORMATION EXERCISES

Clarifying the Concepts

Confirm or Refute

Individually or in groups of two or three carefully review the Introduction and chapter 1 in order to *confirm* or *refute* the following statements. Mark each one "C" or "R" and write the page number where the evidence is to be found. If group discussion follows, be prepared to explain the concepts in your own words and state whether or not you agree with the author.

_____ 1. In many cases when people have tried to explain sanctification they ended up teaching their own particular experiences as the standard for others.

_____ 2. The way to end most of the confusion about sanctification is to bring our doctrines and our interpretations of experience into submission to the Bible.

_____ 3. We must insist that every theological affirmation and every religious claim about sanctification be supported by a literal scripture statement.

_____ 4. The Book of Jeremiah gives us the longest and most thorough treatment of holiness to be found in the New Testament.

_____ 5. Human holiness is derived holiness.

_____ 6. In the Old Testament holiness is separation *from* the unclean *to* the holy God.

_____ 7. Holiness with its emphasis on wholeness and integrity results in our being more human not less human.

_____ 8. Jeremiah and Ezekiel shared the hope that the coming messianic age would bring genuine internal sanctification rather than mere ritualistic holiness.

Exploring Feelings and Appreciations

1. Which of the following comes closest to expressing your feelings when the topic of Christian perfection or entire sanctification is brought up?

A. deep spiritual joy
B. depressing confusion
C. painful memories of past struggles and failures

D. that's something my church believes in, so do I too
E. gratitude for sanctifying grace

2. What concept, statement, or idea in the Introduction or chapter 1 produced the strongest emotional response for you? Was your response positive or negative? Why?

Write a paragraph about your *feelings* after reading this part of the book. If you keep a spiritual life journal, enter your paragraph in it for future reference.

Application to Life

1. After reading the Introduction and chapter 1, what do you want to meditate and pray about?

2. If you were to write a "prayer request list" for yourself in response to this study, what two items would head the list? If you have a "soul friend" with whom you can share openly, consider giving him or her a copy of your "prayer request list."

3. What points in the study relate most directly to your family life? vocational life? devotional life?

4. If you were to try to change *one thing* in your life *this week* in response to this study, what would it be?

2

Sanctification in the New Testament

The Old Testament command, "Be holy, for I am holy" (Lev. 11:44, RSV), takes on new significance in the New Testament. The nature of God is now given clearer definition by the person of Jesus Christ. He is described as the exact image of God (Col. 1:15). If one desires to know what God is like, he looks at the Son of God. Thus the command to be holy as God is holy becomes a call to be Christlike in nature and behavior. In fact, holiness is described in several places in the New Testament in terms of "bearing the family likeness" (see 1 John 2:28 – 3:10).

This same truth can be approached from another direction. In the beginning, God created humans in His own image. The New Testament often suggests that it is God's intention that we be restored to the image that was lost in the Fall. That image is modeled in Jesus.

One of the Early Church fathers illustrated this truth by the story of an artist who painted the picture of a person who sat as a model. But the painting was marred, and the only way it could be adequately redone was for the original to pose again for the artist to paint. The purpose of the Incarnation, said Athanasius, was to make this effaced image visible so that it could be copied anew. In a number of places in the New Testament the term *glory* is a synonym for *image*. For instance, in Rom. 3:23 it is used to identify that from which all persons fall short (see also 2 Cor. 3:18).

Sanctification, then, can best be defined, in the New Testament sense, as the renewal of humanity in the image of God. This theme runs throughout the New Testament Epistles (Rom. 8:28-29; 2 Cor. 3:18). Consistent with the Old Testament hope, the dynamic of this transformation is the Holy Spirit. One thing is clear. The work of the Spirit in the believer's life is to reproduce the character of Christ. It is in terms of this goal that the authentic work of the Spirit is to be recognized and acknowledged (see below).

In the light of this New Testament understanding, we can see the weakness of attempting to define sanctification in terms of psychological states. While growing up in the church I frequently heard preaching that did this. If I had been asked what it meant to be entirely sanctified, I would no doubt have said it meant not "flying off the handle" and throwing a temper tantrum. That was the illustration that was repeatedly used to show how we needed the "second blessing" and the sure evidence we had "it." I see two problems with doing it this way. First, I know people who are even tempered, mild mannered, and gentle toward others in all situations but have no experience of grace at all. Second, clinical psychologists have drugs they can administer to their patients that will alter their behavior. Persons who are susceptible to violent fits of anger can be changed to peaceable, kind, and nonaggressive people. This certainly doesn't take any grace. In a word, if a psychological state is what sanctification is about, the clinical psychologist can sanctify folk. But being conformed to the image of Christ is a completely different matter. Of course, I still believe that "sanctified" folk don't throw temper tantrums. But the truth is, the New Testament says very little about internal psychological states.

In the 18th century John Wesley—father of the modern

holiness movement – was aware of all this, and his interpretation of sanctification is soundly based in Scripture. Thus Mr. Wesley is a safe guide in trying to answer many of the questions we ask but which the New Testament does not directly answer. We shall be referring to his insights as we continue to explore the concept of sanctification.

SPIRITUAL FORMATION EXCERCISES

Clarifying the Concepts

1. The key concepts in this chapter include:
   A. Jesus Christ is the exact image of our holy God.
   B. The New Testament call to holiness is a call to Christlikeness.
   C. Sanctification in the New Testament primarily has to do with our restoration in the image of God, which was marred in the Fall.
   D. The Holy Spirit is the Agent of sanctifying grace, and He reproduces Christlike character in the heart of the sanctified believer.
   E. Sanctification cannot properly be defined in terms of psychological states.

Rank the above "key concepts" in order of their relevance and importance to you right now. If group discussion or sharing with a soul friend is part of your study of this book, be prepared to share the "why" behind your rankings.

2. Who a writer recruits to testify for his cause has a lot to do with the quality of his case. The author of this chapter recruits the following persons to speak for his cause. Evaluate the quality of his "speakers" and identify the concept for which the author asks each of these persons to speak.

   A. Athanasius
   B. The apostle Paul
   C. The apostle John
   D. John Wesley

Exploring Feelings and Appreciations

Browse through this short chapter again and in the margins of your book mark a

+ by any concept or statement that is new to you
? by any point that leaves you puzzled
▼ by any statement or idea that makes you feel depressed, discouraged, or under conviction
▲ by any idea concept or statement that blesses, comforts, inspires, or encourages you

Application to Life

1. Select some of the scriptures cited in this chapter for Bible study. Read them in several translations. Choose one or two to memorize.

2. Select one of the scriptures to use
in family devotions
as this week's table grace
in a letter of spiritual guidance
as something to share with a soul friend
while witnessing to a friend who is ill
as a motto poster for your office or home

3. Identify several hymns that express truths taught in this chapter. Select one as your hymn of the week. Every time a secular song worms its way into your mind this week, push it out and replace it with the holiness hymn of the week.

PART II

Would Someone Please Explain the Doctrine of Sanctification in Terms I Can Understand?

3

Justification and Sanctification

Prior to continuing our inquiry into the meaning of sanctification, we need to explore the meaning of another important theological concept and its relation to sanctification: *justification.* Once again we are presented with a complex picture that needs to be unraveled, and this confusion results from the same situation we saw with the term *sanctification.* The doctrine of justification has been interpreted in different ways by Christians largely because the term *righteousness,* which is the related term, has at least three different uses in Scripture. This varied use has resulted in considerable confusion, even among theologians.

Justification is the term commonly used in theology to refer to the saving relation to God. The sinner or rebel is justified and is thereby acceptable to God. We may thus put the question like this: What does it take to make a person acceptable to God? Two major answers have been given in the history of Christian thought.

The first view interprets justification to mean "to make righteous" and thus confuses it with sanctification. The order then becomes sanctification first and justification next. One must become holy before being accepted by God.

Within this assumption, two ways of becoming holy have been taught. The one that expresses the tendency of human nature to be self-sufficient says that we become righteous on our own. We do good works and thereby earn God's favor. This way has traditionally been identified with the Roman Catholic position. Jesus demonstrated the inadequacy of this approach in His parable of the publican and the Pharisee (Luke 18:9-14). Paul discovered the bankruptcy of this approach through his own experience (Phil. 3:2-10) and actually interpreted the attempt to become one's own savior in this way as an expression of sin (flesh). This way of thinking inevitably results in a belief in purgatory as a place where the process of sanctification can be completed.

The other way of confusing sanctification with justification was first expressed by Augustine in the 4th/5th centuries. He taught that God makes us holy and then accepts us on the basis of that holiness. This is what later developed into the doctrine of works-righteousness in the Middle Ages and became the view described in the previous paragraph.

The second major way of understanding justification is the Protestant way represented by Martin Luther and John Calvin, the major figures in the Protestant Reformation of the 16th century. Here justification precedes sanctification. This means that God accepts us just as we are. He has shown himself willing to forgive by the death of His Son on the Cross. Our part is simply to trust God to keep His word and "accept our acceptance." This is justification by grace through faith. At the moment God accepts us on the basis of His mercy and love, He begins to transform us into the kind of person He intends us to be.

This way of stating it gives us no problem. However, the Reformers interpreted the concept of "righteousness" in a particular way that resulted in an unacceptable conclusion. They understood righteousness as ethical righteousness. While the Catholic view said we must become ethically righteous in order for God to accept us, the Reformers recognized that this undercuts the gospel and makes it good advice, not good news. They said God not only accepts us just as we are but also leaves us that way. In a word, while we are not ethically righteous, God accepts the ethical righteousness of Christ as a substitute righteousness. He treats us *as if* we were righteous when really we are not. But John Wesley correctly objected to this, declaring that God does not fool himself and does not treat us as other than we really are.

Recent biblical scholarship has discovered that there is another way of looking at righteousness. It refers to a relational righteousness. That is, a person is righteous who conforms to the requirements of the relation within which he stands. For instance, being in a family imposes certain obligations upon a person. These do not necessarily have anything to do with ethical righteousness but simply with the relationship.

An interesting example of this is the sordid story in Genesis 38. According to the levirate law, if a husband died without offspring, his brother was required to marry his widow and produce children for him. Tamar, a non-Hebrew, married Judah's son who died, and Judah gave her his next son as her husband according to law. But he, too, died without children, and Judah became nervous about providing his third son. In the subsequent course of events Tamar disguised herself as a prostitute, seduced Judah, and became pregnant by him. But before he departed she required some sign to evidence the fact that Judah was the father and then disappeared. When it became obvious that Tamar was with child, Judah was "righteously" indignant over the immorality of his daughter-in-law and was prepared to have her put to death. But she quickly turned the tables on him by producing the evidence that indicted him. In his response, Judah declared Tamar more "righteous" than he because she lived up to the obligations of the family relation as defined by the levirate law, and he did not. There was nothing ethical in that story. That is why it illustrates this third meaning of righteousness so clearly. Incidentally, Matthew includes Tamar in Jesus' genealogy.

In the Divine-human relation, God's part of the relation is to be faithful to His word. When He does this He is just (righteous). Our part of the relation is to simply take Him at His word, that is, have faith. Meeting our part of the relation constitutes us righteous because we conform to the requirements of the relation. 1 John 1:9 beautifully illustrates this truth: "If we confess our sins, he is faithful and just and will forgive us our sins and purify us from all unrighteousness." "Faithful and just" defines God's righteousness in this context, and our part is simply to accept His offer of forgiveness. We are thereby righteous.

The bottom line is that we do not have to earn God's favor by what we do. Neither do we have to qualify on the basis of some kind of ethical holiness within. We simply take His gracious gift of forgiveness and acceptance. After having received us "just as we are," God begins the process of transforming us into the kind of persons He intended us to be. And this divine intention is embodied in the doctrine of the image of God. *That* is what sanctification is all about.

SPIRITUAL FORMATION EXERCISES

Clarifying the Concepts

For Reflection

1. The main question addressed in this chapter on *justification* is, "What does it take to make a person acceptable to God?" In one sentence, state the author's answer to this question.

2. The author discusses three kinds of righteousness: works righteousness, substitute righteousness, relational righteousness.

Which of the three most resembles what you were taught as a child? What persons or groups teach the three kinds of righteousness? Read this chapter over again. Restate the definitions of justification and righteousness until you could explain them to a 12-year-old child.

3. Study the Article of Faith in the Nazarene *Manual* called "Justification, Regeneration, and Adoption" (p. 33, para. 9-12, 1989 edition).

4. Study the scriptures cited in this chapter: Luke 18:9-14; Phil. 3:2-10; 1 John 1:9. Write a paragraph about what these passages say about what it takes to make a person acceptable to God.

Exploring Feelings and Appreciations

It is not unusual for those who hunger and thirst for sanctifying grace to devalue what God has already done for them in saving, that is, justifying grace. But being born from above, regenerated, justified, and adopted into the family of God is glorious news. Even if you are not as yet fully sanctified, take time now to thank and praise God for justifying grace. Celebrate saving grace, knowing that sanctifying grace will surely come. One of Charles Wesley's greatest hymns celebrated saving grace.

And can it be that I should gain
An int'rest in the Saviour's blood!
Died He for me, who caused His pain?
For me, who Him to death pursued?
Amazing love! How can it be
That Thou, my God, shouldst die for me?

He left His Father's throne above,
So free, so infinite His grace!
Emptied himself of all but love,
And bled for Adam's helpless race.
'Tis mercy all, immense and free!
For, O my God, it found out me!

Long my imprisoned spirit lay,
Fast bound in sin and nature's night.
Thine eyes diffused a quick'ning ray.
I woke; the dungeon flamed with light.
My chains fell off; my heart was free.
I rose, went forth, and followed Thee.

Justifying grace is not something trivial; it is something glorious. It is more than a mere prelude to sanctification.

Prayerfully contemplate the preceding song. After reflecting on the hymn and your own conversion experience, try to write your own additional verse to this song. All right, so you are not a poet—at least list some ideas or images you would use if you were to write a song celebrating your conversion experience.

Application to Life

Sanctification begins in justification. Dunning expresses it this way, "After having received us 'just as we are' God begins the process of transforming us into the kind of persons He intended us to be." Some have called this initial sanctification. The justified believer becomes the object of sanctifying grace. This favorite prayer of Wesley's (taken from the Anglican liturgy) belongs on every justified believer's lips.

Almighty God, unto whom all hearts be open,
All desires, known, and from whom no secrets are hid:
Cleanse the thoughts of our hearts
By the inspiration of thy Holy Spirit,
That we may perfectly love thee,
And worthily magnify thy holy name,
Through Jesus Christ our Lord, Amen.

This prayer is a near-perfect outline of John Wesley's doctrine of entire sanctification. Pray it, memorize it. Write it on the back of your business card or on something else that you can tuck in your wallet or purse. Pray this prayer every time you think of it. Share it with a prayer partner. The results could be dramatic.

4

Sanctification and the Image of God

John Wesley said, "Ye know that the great end of religion is, to renew our hearts in the image of God, to repair that total loss of righteousness and true holiness which we sustained by the sin of our first parents. Ye know that all religion which does not answer this end, all that stops short of this, the renewal of our soul in the image of God, after the likeness of Him that created it, is no other than a poor farce, and a mere mockery of God, to the destruction of our own soul."[5]

While a number of attempts have been made to explain what it means for human persons to be in God's image, a careful study of the relevant biblical material has led most contemporary interpreters to the conclusion that it consists of a fourfold relation. It is constituted by a *relation to God* that includes obedience, openness, and love. It includes also a *relation to other persons* that is sincere, loving, and open. It furthermore implies a responsible stewardship in *relation to possessions* and finally a *relation of submission* of oneself to the Creator that recognizes the place of the self in the Divine-human relation. We acknowledge ourselves as servants and not sovereigns in our world.

All these relations were disrupted by the disobedience

of the first pair, and all of us since have come into the world with all these relations distorted by an innate self-centeredness. This is why egocentricity is identified by classical Christian theology as the essence of sin.

As we read through the Bible, we see that God's redemptive purpose is continuously focused on these relations. Thus His redemptive program always has sanctifying implications. We can see this when we look at this intention as it is embodied in the law, the Sermon on the Mount, and the New Testament Epistles.

The Law. The first and perhaps most important thing we need to learn about the law is that God did not give it as a means to be saved. The people of Israel in the Old Testament did not become the people of God because they kept the rules. Rather they became the people of God through His act of deliverance, an act that was based on His faithfulness to His promises. Afterward, the law entered the picture as the divine will for the way God's people were to live out that deliverance. The law was to be observed in loving response to grace.

The law addressed all the relations that we suggested above made up the image of God. When the law was obeyed, the people lived out their destiny as persons made in the divine image.

When Moses summarized the whole law in Deut. 6:5, he did so in terms of love, specifically loving God with all one's heart, soul, and strength. And Lev. 19:18 summarizes the law's teaching about relations to others by exhorting, "Thou shalt love they neighbour as thyself" (KJV). Furthermore, the law gives extensive guidance as to the appropriate way to relate to the land, over which the people were to exercise responsible stewardship.

The Sermon on the Mount. The collection of teachings commonly referred to as the Sermon on the Mount is a description of life within the kingdom of God. It, too, embodies Jesus' teaching about the divine intention for Kingdom people in terms of all the relations in which they stand. A great experience is to work carefully through the sermon to identify the fourfold relation, repeatedly addressed.

The Epistles. The letters of the New Testament, especially those written by Paul, abound with references and implications about God's intention to renew humans in God's image. The unique feature here is the recognition that this image is embodied in Jesus Christ. Thus the image of God and the image of Christ become synonymous. Holiness is understood as Christlikeness.

SPIRITUAL FORMATION EXERCISES

Clarifying the Concepts

You are the teacher:

Suppose that you have to teach a Sunday School class a lesson on "Holiness as Restoration of the Image of God in Humankind." Study this chapter thoroughly. Then study the Sermon on the Mount (Matthew 5–7), to which the author refers, noting the four dimensions of being in the image of God. Then prepare your lesson. Begin by setting your objectives. You can do this by answering these three questions:

What do I want them to know or understand?
What do I want them to feel and appreciate?
What do I want them to do about it?

Exploring Feelings and Values

Being in the image of God means a relationship

1. to God characterized by obedience, openness, and love
2. to other people characterized by sincerity, openness, and love
3. to possessions characterized by responsible stewardship
4. of submission to the Creator

From the following list record the feeling(s) produced by each of the four relationships that pertain to being in the image of God.

A. gratitude
B. hope
C. fear
D. condemnation
E. let us pray
F. relief
G. other:

Application to Life

1. Discovering the Gap

On a scale of 1 to 10 rate yourself on each of the four relationships highlighted in this chapter: relation to God, to others, to possessions, and the submission of yourself to the Creator. (1 equals very dissatisfied in this area, 10 means fully satisfied in this area.)

1___ 2___ 3___ 4___ 5___ 6___ 7___ 8___ 9___ 10___

Next, using the same scale mark where you would like to be by this time next year.

By doing this you have discovered the gap between where you are and where you would like to be in regard to these very important relationships.

2. Bridging the Gap

Remember that when it comes to sanctifying grace much of what happens to us is up to our Sovereign Lord who leads and moves at the right times in the right directions. But there is much for us to do in responding to the God who calls us to live a holy, Christlike life. As you examine the gap between where you are and where your best self longs to be, do you hear the voice of God calling you to bridge that gap?

What do you think the Lord wants you to do to close the gap this month, this week, today? Make a list, be specific. Pray for grace and strength to properly respond to the upward call of God in Christ. After all, holiness is Christlikeness.

5

Sanctification and the Spirit

As we saw in our comments on sanctification in the Old Testament, the hope arose that in the age to come when God's Spirit would be poured out on all God's children, there would be inward moral renewal. The New Testament opens with the claim, made both explicitly and implicitly, that this hope has now become a reality.

The New Testament, however, presents us with an interesting picture. The understanding of the experience of the Spirit undergoes significant development. Not only is there an advance beyond the Old Testament understanding, but within the New Testament itself a clear pattern emerges. This pattern gives us important light on the relation between the Holy Spirit and sanctification.

Let us trace this development in broad strokes. First, it is apparent that the Gospel writers are attempting to convey the message that there is a unique relation between Jesus and the Spirit. His birth is the result of the Spirit's activity. He is endowed with the Spirit at His baptism, and His entire ministry is carried out in the power of the Spirit. But unlike the prophets of the Old Testament, whose work was also Spirit anointed, His endowment with the Spirit is permanent and without measure. The Fourth Gospel becomes very explicit. The giving of the Spirit to believers in the new age awaits the completion of Jesus' ministry. Why is that the case?

E. Stanley Jones helps us with his keen insight here:

> If the power of the Spirit was to be Christlike power, then it was necessary to see that power manifested through the whole gamut of life, from a carpenter's bench to the throne of the universe, from the denial, betrayal, and crucifixion on the one hand to the triumph of the resurrection on the other. For we had to see this power manifested on a cross as forgiveness of enemies; and we had to see it manifested as supreme modesty and humility, which when he triumphed over his enemies in the resurrection, made him refuse to appear in triumph before them to cow and overwhelm them—he was humble in every circumstance, and yet almighty in this humility. We had to see this power in its total range, for it was universal power.[6]

In a word, Jesus' experience of the Spirit gave content to His followers' experience of the Spirit. The implications of this are radical. No longer is power to be understood in terms of overwhelming force but as the power of suffering love. And this is how the work of the Spirit is to be understood in His sanctifying activity in the believer's life. The purpose of the infilling of the Spirit is to transform life into Christlikeness.

It took quite a while for the Early Church to understand this. And like them, we still have not learned it very well.

Paul had the greatest influence in teaching the distinctly *Christian* experience of the sanctifying Spirit. He encountered a sub-Christian manifestation of spiritual experience at Corinth and sought to correct it without denying that the persons involved were believers. Their understanding needed to be corrected. They thought the Spirit's presence was validated by the presence of gifts, especially spectacular ones like speaking in tongues. But Paul insisted that the true evidence was the presence of love in all its radical Christlikeness (1 Corinthians 13).

James Stewart speaks for New Testament scholarship in general when he says: "In the primitive Christian community there was a tendency at the first—perhaps quite natural under the circumstances—to revert to the cruder conceptions of the Spirit and to trace His working mainly in such phenomena as speaking in tongues. It was Paul who saved the nascent faith from that dangerous retrogression."[7]

The implication of this is that the normative and distinctly Christian experience of the Spirit is found more in the fruit of the Spirit than in the gifts of the Spirit. The latter are genuine and important but may be duplicated. The 19th-century theologian F. Schleiermacher put it both beautifully and accurately when he said, "The fruits of the Spirit are nothing but the virtues of Christ."

What, then, is the relation of sanctification and the Spirit? The Spirit serves many functions as the Agent of God's work in the world, but in His sanctifying function He indwells the believer to produce within him and in his life the character of Jesus Christ.

SPIRITUAL FORMATION EXERCISES

Clarifying the Concept

The key concept powerfully taught in this chapter is that the sanctifying Spirit comes to make radical changes in our lives. He produces in us the radical virtues of Christ, such as

Radical humility

Radical forgiveness

Radical love

Radical power (the power of suffering love, not force)

Radical Christlikeness

Radical Christlikeness in Real Life

Three True Stories

JERRY AND HANNAH

Jerry and Hannah had been married for four years when Jerry entered military service. He was stationed in Okinawa. When his term of service ended he chose to sign up for another term in Okinawa rather than come home. Hannah was justly worried. Soon she discovered that Jerry had been living with a local woman. They now had a child. He wanted them, not Hannah. He wrote and asked for a divorce. Hannah was devastated. She waited, then several months later she received word that Jerry had died from a quick-acting cancer. As time passed Hannah found Jerry's live-in and their child often in her mind. She prayed about them.

What was she to do?

She certainly owed nothing to this woman who had stolen her husband, did she?

Her friend advised her to forget them and Jerry and make a new life for herself.

What would you have advised her to do?

What would you have done if you were in her shoes?

Through military contacts Hannah traced down the woman and child. They were destitute, living in slum conditions. Hannah went through all the red tape and made the financial sacrifices necessary to bring woman and child to America and took them into her own home. Hannah worked in a factory, and the Okinawan woman kept the house. Together they raised the child of the man who had wronged them both.

ENRIQUE PEDROZA

A 16-year-old young man walked along a road near his father's farm in a Central American country. Three government soldiers confronted him and accused him of being a revolutionary guerrilla. After all, they reasoned, he was old enough to join the army. Since he had not he must be a guerrilla or be in sympathy with their cause. They tied him to a tree, stripped him, beat him, cut off his genitals with a machette, and finally tortured him to death.

Enrique Pedroza, the victim's father, found his dead son.

What should he do? Get his gun and seek revenge?
Go to court to seek justice? Join the guerrillas?
Let his hatred keep him warm waiting for the chance to not only get even but also get ahead?

What would you advise?
What would you do if your son had been slaughtered?

The following Sunday Enrique stood to teach his Sunday School class of men and women from his village. "To be like Jesus," he said, "we must forgive our enemies. Not just on the outside, but from the heart. If revenge is right, then Jesus was wrong. I want to be like Jesus. Let us pray for our enemies who hate us and sometimes destroy us."

Is this the radical forgiveness that the sanctifying Spirit brings?

Hilda, the Nurse

Hilda worked in a psychiatric hospital. She really cared for her patients. One of them was a 12-year-old girl named Tammy who stayed in a padded room. Tammy had been raised by alcoholic parents who hated, abused, and beat her. One day as she stood screaming her mother took a shotgun and killed her father. Tammy's mind snapped. She went into uncontrollable violent behavior. Nothing they did at the hospital could get through to her. Finally the doctors decided that the only hope for Tammy was a catharsis in which the girl could vent and exhaust her anger on someone. Hilda volunteered. Every day she went into the padded cell with this violent patient and absorbed her scratching and pounding and hair pulling until the girl was exhausted. Every day just as she left she would turn to Tammy with her own blood streaming down her face and say, "Darling, I love you. Darling, I love you." Suffering love began to win after two weeks and Tammy had hope again.

The sanctifying Spirit comes to produce in us radical Christlikeness, that is to say, radical love, radical humility, radical forgiveness, radical unselfishness, radical suffering love. Do you have the nerve to openly invite Him into your heart in His fullness? How shall you begin your prayer?

6

Sanctification and Perfection

Perfection is a term that is used in many contexts, but when it is used as a religious term we immediately get nervous. And well we should, if by it we mean "without flaw" or "full" or "complete, needing no improvement." But is this the way it is used in Scripture? Let's look at some scriptural evidence.

The first time the term appears in our English Bibles is in Gen. 6:9 where Noah is described as "a just man and perfect in his generations" (KJV). All the modern translations avoid the term *perfect* in favor of *blameless.* We will note this issue in a moment, but for the present we need simply to be aware that there seems to be a significant qualification of *perfection* in the phrase "in his generations." This appears to imply that it is a relative perfection ascribed to Noah, related to the light or knowledge he had in that primitive time. No suggestion of "completeness" or "absoluteness" is found here.

The second use of the term is found in Gen. 17:1 where the Lord appeared to Abram and said, "I am the Almighty God; walk before me, and be thou perfect" (KJV). As in the first reference, we used the King James because most modern translations render it "blameless" (NIV, RSV, NEB). The reason for this in both references is that the Septuagint (Greek translation of the Old Testament) rendered the Hebrew word *tamin* into a Greek word meaning "blameless." While this was no doubt an attempt to avoid the onus of the term *perfect,* it is unacceptable as a translation.

What does the Hebrew word *tamin* mean? Good scholarship points out that it refers to a relational perfection toward God. It does not necessarily mean moral perfection as one living without mistakes, but "it signifies complete, unqualified surrender." The same word is used in Deut. 20:5 to refer to relations among men with the sense of "without ulterior motives, unreserved."[8] It further carries the meaning of "openness" and "wholeness." All these reflect a "perfect" relation with God.

At the conclusion of Jesus' exhortation to the citizens of the kingdom of heaven to show disinterested love as God does, He says: "Be perfect, therefore, as your heavenly Father is perfect" (Matt. 5:48). This command/promise disturbs a lot of people. Perhaps the simplest way to understand it is to say that just as God functions as God, His disciples are to function as disciples. "Perfect" is related to performing according to one's situation and purpose. A perfect Christian is not a perfect God but is subject to all the limitations and shortcomings of finitude, including mistakes and blunders. It is for this reason that John Wesley insisted that one should always speak of *Christian* perfection—an important qualification.

One of the most important passages for understanding the biblical concept of perfection is found in Phil. 3:12-15. In the course of these four verses Paul both denies and claims perfection. In verse 12 he denies that he is "already perfect" but declares his intention to "press on to make it my own, because Christ Jesus has made me his own" (RSV). What is this perfection the apostle is pursuing with all his being? It seems to be conformity to the character of Christ, a receding goal that will always be out before him as a tantalizing ideal. But the fascinating thing about the "perfection" (translated "maturity" in NIV and RSV) he unpretentiously claims is that it is marked by the pursuit of the perfection he denies. This is a thrilling insight. Perfection is thus not attainment but pursuit. It is not static but dynamic. It is with this truth in mind that John Wesley denied there was any "perfection of degrees" as he called it, that is, one that does not know of continual increase.

One final scriptural reference may be found in the Book of Hebrews, where *perfection* is a key word. It is used here with the same dynamic significance that characterizes the other uses we have examined. It is a bit startling to hear the author speak of Jesus being made perfect through suffering and obedience (2:10; 5:9; 7:28). But that is one of the most important clues to its meaning. The term is used to refer to a heavenly tabernacle (9:11) and to Jesus' self-sacrifice that perfects those who are "being sanctified" (10:14; 12:23).

These references enable us to see quite clearly how the writer of the letter is using the concept of perfection. It is a term pertaining to function as we suggested in connection with Jesus' command to "be perfect." Jesus being perfected relates to the carrying out of the mission for which, as the Son, God sent Him into the world. This mission called for perfect obedience to the Father's will and could only be consummated by His suffering on the Cross.

By analogy, the perfecting (or perfection of) believers involves their realization of the purpose for which God called them into His kingdom. It does not imply any "finished" or finalized condition signifying absence of flaws but something far more dynamic and realistic. We should fear the stagnation that might result from a claim to be "perfect" in any other sense.

The central question then is, Is such a perfection possible for human beings in this life? That is the unique emphasis of the Wesleyan reading of biblical revelation. Following John Wesley, we believe the answer to the question is yes. Mr. Wesley based his optimism concerning the possibilities of grace in this regard on four foundation stones.

The first of these four is the *promise* of perfection in Scripture, or the promise of complete deliverance from all sin. Numerous examples may be found in both the Old and New Testaments. Wesley includes among his references Deut. 30:6; Ps. 130:8; Ezek. 36:25, 29; Rom. 8:3-4; 2 Cor. 7:1; Eph. 5:25-27; 1 John 3:8.

In addition there are *prayers* for perfection such as the petition in the Lord's Prayer, "deliver us from evil." If Wesley had known the Jewish background of this prayer, he would have found even stronger support than he imagined. The corollary to this petition found in the Jewish Talmud is an explicit prayer for deliverance from the sin principle found in the human heart. In a word, it is not so much a prayer for deliverance from outward harm as a prayer for inward holiness. Wesley also includes among the prayers John 17:20-23; Eph. 3:14; and 1 Thess. 5:23.

There are also *commands* in Scripture to the same effect, such as Matt. 4:48 and 22:37. Furthermore, several *examples* may be found in the Bible. In addition to those mentioned in the early part of this section, one could mention (and Wesley does) John and refers to 1 John 4:17.

The reasoning behind these arguments is simple and clear. The four bases are really promises. Prayers, commands, and examples are what Wesley would call "covered" promises, or we might say implicit promises. The assumption is that what the Lord inspired persons to pray for He will answer; what He commands He will perform; and the fact that certain persons have experienced full salvation is an implicit promise that all may. Thus the basis is the faithfulness of God in keeping His word. For this reason Wesley made much of the definition of faith in Heb. 11:1—"Now faith is the substance of things hoped for, the evidence of things not seen" (KJV). He believed that what God offered (promised) one could depend on to become reality and even act as if it had already taken place. You could "take it to the bank." Hence his "optimism of grace" was based on confidence in the divine faithfulness and power, not upon human capacity.

In addition to these four foundations, Wesley also added to his arsenal those scriptures that spoke of present salvation. He refers to Titus 2:11-14 and Luke 1:69. Numerous others could be added that would support the idea that God's provision is for present deliverance from sin and not simply for future deliverance at or beyond death.

One could go further and suggest an additional basis of confidence in the possibility of present full salvation: the atonement of Jesus Christ. If anything is clear from the New Testament, it is that in the Cross and the Resurrection Jesus triumphed over evil, sin, and the devil. Thus He broke their power within our history, in our here and now. If His victory through His death and resurrection was this decisive, it is reasonable to think that the "power of the resurrection" (Phil. 3:10) thereby released in the world can conquer sin in human life.

The poet adequately expressed it thus:

My sin—not in part, but the whole—
Is nailed to His cross
And I bear it no more.
Praise the Lord, praise the Lord, O my soul.

—H. G. Spafford

SPIRITUAL FORMATION EXERCISES

Clarifying the Concepts

1. Define Christian perfection as it is described in this chapter. Be brief, using no more than two sentences.

2. Examine and evaluate the scriptural foundation for perfection as found in the *promises, prayers, commands,* and *examples* of the Bible.

3. Study Phil. 3:12-15.

4. Since the term *perfection* means so many different things, perhaps we should just stop using it. If you think this is a good idea, what term would you suggest be substituted for it?

5. Respond to these statements referring to real-life examples, observations, and personal experiences to clarify the issue when possible.

A. Perfection is more about pursuit than about attainment.

B. The phrase in the Lord's Prayer "deliver us from evil" in its Talmudic origins was a prayer for deliverance from the sin principle in the human heart.

C. Christian perfection has more to do with divine faithfulness than human capacity.

D. The crucifixion and resurrection of Jesus signifies that He broke the power of sin and death in the here and now.

Exploring Feelings and Attitudes

Write a letter to the author of this book. Let him know exactly what feelings and emotions this chapter stirred or soothed in you. Be specific. Hold nothing back.

Were you surprised that you had such strong feelings about this subject?

Application to Life

1. If there is one person that I know who is an example of Christian perfection it is ______________________.

2. This person's most Christlike behaviors are ________ ____ ____.

3. The personal traits that I most admire in this individual are ____ ____.

4. The biggest difference between me and this example of Christian perfection is ______________________________ ____.

5. If you asked this person to spend time with you talking about spiritual things, what do you think his or her response would be?

7

Sanctification, Love, and Sin

Sanctification has both a positive and a negative side. On the negative side it is deliverance from inward sin. On the positive side it is generally understood in terms of "love" with *entire* sanctification being "perfect love." In this section, we want to explore the concept of holiness in terms of love.[9]

From the beginning of Christian thinking about holiness in human experience, it has been interpreted in terms of love. When John Wesley spoke of love as the sum of Christian sanctification[10] he was fully in accord with the heart of classical Christian teaching on the subject.

Speaking of holiness in terms of love enables us to adequately answer many questions that are raised by the seeker after truth. Let us examine some of these questions with suggested responses.

When does sanctification begin? If it is equated with love, it begins with the first response to grace in the human heart. As John Wesley said, "From the moment we are justified, till we give up our spirits to God, love is the fulfilling of the law; of the whole evangelical law, which took place of the Adamic law, when the first promise of 'the seed of the woman' was made. Love . . . is the one *kind* of holiness, which is found, only in various *degrees*, in believers who are distinguished by St. John into 'little children, young men, and fathers.'"[11]

If this is the case, what, then, is the difference between the experience of those who have been entirely sanctified and those who have not? The difference is that in the one, love is mixed with love of self, love of the world, and love of things other than God alone. In the entirely sanctified, love is unmixed. In fact, one could say that sanctification is "love expelling sin." This helps define the sin that remains in the believer who is not yet entirely sanctified. It is defective love, or love not fully perfected, that is, not fully focused on its proper object.

How, then, should entire sanctification be defined? In the light of our discussion thus far we can see clearly how appropriate it is to define entire sanctification as loving God with one's whole heart, soul, mind, and strength and one's neighbor as oneself.

This truth is stated simply by Wesley in the context of another important issue. To the question, "How shall we avoid setting perfection too high or too low?" he answers like this: "By keeping to the Bible, and setting it just as high as the Scripture does. It is nothing higher and nothing lower than this, – the pure love of God and man; the loving God with all our heart and soul, and our neighbor as ourselves. It is love governing the heart and life, running through all our tempers, words, and actions."[12]

In fact, Wesley insisted that love was the great goal of God's saving work in human life. Faith is the means by which we are restored to God's favor, but the end of faith is love. No wonder that he borrowed Paul's phrase in Gal. 5:6, "Faith working through love" (RSV), to describe the nature of the Christian life. "Faith," he said, "is the grand means of restoring that holy love wherein man was originally created."[13]

What, then, does it mean to love God with all our heart, soul, mind, and strength? Once again, Wesley's answer is illuminating and helpful. "But what is it to love God? Is not to love anything the same as habitually to delight in it? Is not, then, the purport of both these injunctions this, – that we delight in the Creator more than His creatures; that we take more pleasure in Him than in anything He has made, and rejoice in nothing so much as in serving Him."[14]

This is no doubt a commentary on the fact that Wesley always identified the Pauline trilogy as evidence that one was entirely sanctified: "Rejoice evermore, pray without ceasing, in every thing give thanks." Where these qualities are present they are indications of great joy in the presence of God. Certainly this is an evidence of love for God.

The negative side of this truth is that love of the created world or any aspect of it is always to be subordinate to love of God. As many, beginning with Augustine, have said, "We should love God and use things, whereas we are prone to love things and use God." It is a question of priorities.

In his essay on *The Character of a Methodist*, those who have been perfected in love are described by Wesley in these words: "God is the joy of his heart, and the desire of his soul; which is constantly crying out, 'whom have I in heaven but thee? And there is none upon earth that I desire beside thee! My God and my all! Thou art the strength of my heart, and my portion forever!"[15]

But love for God also means obedience to His will. As Jesus said, "If you love me, you will keep my commandments" (John 14:15, RSV). This is the flip side of the truth that the essence of sin is seeking one's own way without regard for God's will.

It seems important in this connection to note the significance of distinguishing between the attitude of obedience and the specific knowledge of what obedience involves. Obedience cannot occur as behavior in the abstract, only in terms of specifics. And we cannot with certainty identify what such obedience might mean for others, only for ourselves. It is true that there are specific biblical commands, but even these must be known in order to be obeyed. This is why it is necessary to emphasize that obedience is an attitude and should not be confused with a particular performance—at least for others.

Then enters the second commandment as definitive, for Wesleyan thought, of perfect love. It should be said that love for neighbor is the fruit of love of God. What does it mean to love one's neighbor as oneself? I believe the key here is to identify the nature of the love that is enjoined by the second commandment. Most readers will recognize the term *agape* that is the distinctive New Testament word here. Contrary to much popular interpretation, agape is a love that does not involve emotion. It could be defined as "outgoing concern," the will to seek the well-being of the object of love. Wesley referred to it as "universal benevolence," "a sincere, tender, disinterested love for all mankind."[16]

Only in this way can love be commanded, since even God cannot reasonably command an emotion. Understood like this, you can love someone you don't necessarily like. One can love enemies as well as friends in terms of seeking their well-being.

This character of agape enables us to have a better grasp of the possible implication of the second commandment that there is a legitimate love of self, "love your neighbor *as yourself.*" This probably means that we are asked to seek the same well-being for others that we seek for ourselves. In any case, we must admit the difficulty of explaining exactly how this fits in. Thinkers throughout the history of Christian thought have differed considerably on the matter. But since we are following the guidance of Wesley, we should listen to some of his observations regarding self-love.

He argues that proper self-love is not "a Sin" but "an indisputable duty."[17] Man has an obligation to love himself in the same way that he has an obligation to love God and neighbor. Unregulated (inordinate) self-love is an expression of sin, consequently we may infer that proper self-love is regulated love.[18]

At a very practical level, Wesley addresses a question that would inevitably arise when one considers a possible conflict between self-love and other-love. How should one utilize his resources in this situation? In his treatment of Christian stewardship in a sermon on *The Use of Money* he says:

> The directions which God has given us, touching the use of our worldly substance, may be comprised in the following particulars. If you desire to be a faithful and a wise steward, out of that portion of your Lord's goods which He has for the present lodged in your hands, but with the right of resuming whenever it pleases Him, first, provide things needful for yourself; food to eat, raiment to put on, whatever nature moderately requires for preserving the body in health and strength. Secondly, provide these for your wife, your children, your servants, or any others who pertain to your household. If, when this is done, there be an overplus left, then "do good to them that are of the household of faith." If there be an overplus still, "as you have opportunity, do good unto all men." In so doing, you give all you can; nay, in a sound sense, all you have: for all that is laid out in this manner is really given to God. You "render unto God the things that are God's," not only by what you give to the poor, but also by that which you expend in providing things needful for yourself and your household.[19]

The distinctions Wesley makes in these instructions are based on a proper balance between a "regulated" self-love and an "inordinate" self-love. This distinction cannot be legislated, certainly not in specifics. It is spiritually discerned and that by the one involved, not an external observer. Here is no doubt one reason why Wesley insisted that apart from a special gift of discernment, we cannot tell as a spectator if another person is "perfected in love."

Wesley, along with the New Testament, recognized the legitimacy of different degrees of love in relation to various groups. This has been pictured as a series of concentric circles.

The outer circle refers to mankind in general including enemies as well as strangers about whom we know nothing. The second, smaller circle includes those who are part of the Christian community worldwide, those who love God. The inner circle includes those who belong to the same congregation and in whose company one receives the means of grace. W. M. Greathouse would add to this an even more central circle defined by the family, "our nearest neighbors." The difference here is a difference in the degree of love. One might also add that there is an increasing measure of those kinds of love that involve warmth and friendship as one moves toward the inner circle.

We have looked at the positive side of sanctification, the renewal of love. Now we must turn to the negative side, the removal of sin. To do this adequately we must briefly address the question of the nature of sin.

The first point to observe is that sin is recognized throughout the Bible as well as in Christian theology as being twofold in nature. Simply put, it refers to what we do and what we are. If God is to deal adequately with the sin question in human life, both dimensions must be addressed.

The essence of sin is love locked into a wrong center.[20] Human persons were created to love God, and the elevation of something less than God to the place of ultimacy in one's life perverts that created destiny. Thus when Adam and Eve chose to attempt to become their own God, they were guilty of idolatry. And since it was the self that was to be sovereign, it was the idolatry of self. In a word, we may identify the essence of sin as self-centeredness or self-sovereignty.

In the unconverted state, persons live by the dominant motive of self-will. This is what Paul means by "living according to the flesh" (Rom. 8:5, 12, RSV), and to which he refers in Rom. 6:13: "Do not yield your members to sin as instruments of wickedness" (RSV), and verse 19, "just as you once yielded your members to impurity and to greater and greater iniquity" (RSV). This point is made explicitly in Eph. 2:3 where the author is describing the condition of persons outside of Christ.[21]

In the new birth, God "breaks the power of cancelled sin and sets the prisoner free," but the being of sin remains. This means that the believer no longer lives by the primary motivation of self-sovereignty, but he soon discovers that the tendency in this direction has survived the initial work of grace. There are attitudes and dispositions contrary to the mind that was in Christ that if yielded to would result in unchristian behaviors. In the experience of many there is a struggle between the "flesh" (the self-centered existence) and the Spirit within us who yearns jealously for our undivided love (James 4:5). The hymn writer captured this experience of the divided mind in the words, "Prone to wander, Lord I feel it, / Prone to leave the God I love."

But the "reason the Son of God appeared was to destroy the works of the devil" (1 John 3:8, RSV), and the provisions of the Atonement include not only the remedy for the acts of sin but also the healing of the perverted love that we all experience by virtue of being "in Adam."

SPIRITUAL FORMATION EXERCISES

Clarifying the Concepts

Examine, define, explain, and evaluate these key phrases from chapter 7:

1. love—the positive side of sanctification
2. sin removal—the negative side of sanctification
3. unmixed love—the mark of the sanctified
4. love expelling sin
5. love God—use things
6. obedience as "flip side"
7. regulated self-love

8. agape as love of neighbor
9. love locked into a wrong center
10. "prone to wander, Lord, I feel it"

Exploring Values

The essence of entire sanctification is loving God above anyone or anything else. In short, it is to love God with all your heart, soul, mind, and strength. Surely this would be a most basic **value** for Christians. But is it a value, or something less? The values clarification people say that for something to be properly labeled a **value** it must be something that (1) the person repeatedly does, (2) is prized and cherished, (3) is chosen from among alternatives, (4) the person publicly affirms, and (5) affects the decisions and behavior of the person under consideration. To find out whether or not supreme love for God is a value or something less for you, respond to this quiz.

1. Do you repeatedly state and demonstrate that loving God is a supreme value for you? ____ Yes ____ No

2. Is your love for God something you treasure and cherish? ____ Yes ____ No

3. Was your love for God freely chosen from among alternatives? ____ Yes ____ No

4. Do you gladly and publicly affirm your love for God even when people might dislike or persecute you? ____ Yes ____ No

5. Does your love for God govern your decisions and behaviors? ____ Yes ____ No

Application to Life

1. Love others as much as you love yourself.

The second dimension of sanctified love is love for our neighbor. Christianity has always taught that we must love others just as much as we love ourselves.

Think about John Wesley's counsel on loving others:

> Thou shalt love thy neighbour. ... Thou shalt embrace with the most tender good will, the most earnest and cordial affection, the most inflamed desires of preventing or removing all evil, and of procuring for him every possible good. *Thy neighbour*—that is, not only thy friend, thy kinsman ... not only the virtuous, the friendly, him that loves thee, that ... returns thy kindness, but every ... human creature, every soul which God hath made; not excepting ... him that thou knowest to be evil and unthankful, him that ... persecutes thee: him thou shalt love as thyself; with the same invariable thirst after his happiness ... the same unwearied care to screen him from whatever might grieve or hurt either his soul or body *(The Way to the Kingdom)*.

2. You may want to memorize and pray these prayers extracted from John Wesley's own handwritten prayer journal:

Grant that I may look upon the defeats of my neighbour as if they were my own. ... Almighty God ... teach me to have compassion for the weaknesses and frailties of my brethren; to put the best construction on all their actions; to interpret all doubtful things to their advantage, and cheerfully bear with their real infirmities.

3. Proper self-love is a Christian duty.

In this chapter we are taught that proper self-love is not a "sin" but an "indisputable duty." This is good news for those who have been told that true submission to God requires us to despise ourselves.

Consider this: Your worth is stated and restated in the Bible. You are an object of divine love. God loves you unconditionally. **Who are you to hate what God loves?**

PART III

What Does Sanctification Look Like in Life and Religious Experience?

8

Sanctification and Experience

It is one thing to develop a doctrine. It is another to realize that doctrine in experience. Thus it is important to attempt to understand how the biblical teaching about sanctification applies to daily life.

Perhaps the first step is to explore what the Bible says about experience. But before we can do that, we must try to define what the term *experience* means.

For our purposes in this essay, we will use *experience* to refer to the manner in which sanctifying grace operates in human life, how it is actualized in our daily, down-to-earth existence. The first question, then, to be addressed is, Is there a revealed pattern of this divine action?

It is important to recognize that the Bible does not lay down a stereotyped answer to this question. We may find hints concerning our role in the process, but none of these suggests a formula that can become a ritual. One reason for this is that sanctification is the work of God, and He cannot be forced into a box. Another is the irreducible variety of religious experiences. It is true that some spiritual leaders have laid down "steps to sanctification" and attempted to describe the manner in which God works, but this raises a real danger of creating clones of their personal experience and fails to recognize the sovereignty of God as well as the influence of many forces on the shape of experience. In addition, the Bible does not prescribe a pattern of how God invariably works in human life. It basically describes the state of humanity in sin and sets forth the goal of God's redemptive process but does not specify the specific route by which one would arrive there.

John Wesley is at his best when he discusses this aspect of sanctification. He recognized the truth that the Bible is silent on the manner, and he attempted to examine the experiences of as many people as he could who claimed to have experienced the grace of entire sanctification. By this method he came to conclusions about how God *normally* worked but not how He *must* work. What did he discover by this inductive method?

He learned that sanctification is a lifelong process that includes an instantaneous moment at which one is perfected in love. To this moment he gave the term *entire sanctification* or *Christian perfection,* or *full salvation.* This moment occurs when God cuts short His work in righteousness and delivers the believer from all sin. He also discovered from experience what was quite explicit in the structure of the New Testament: No one had experienced full deliverance from inward sin at the moment of initial salvation. While it may not have been apparent at first due to the joy and victory of conversion, eventually all became aware of remaining sin (self-centeredness).

The lifelong process is not difficult to establish since the New Testament references to the Christian life are dominantly in the present progressive tense in the original Greek. This Mr. Wesley understood as that gradual renewal in the image of God that begins in the new birth and continues until death—and beyond.

Because of this *obvious* teaching of Scripture, the whole-life developmental aspect of sanctification has been recognized by almost all Christian teachers. But the distinctive that Wesley discovered in the experience of many was that there was the possibility of deliverance from all sin *in this life* and that this stage of grace occurs in a moment of time.

He based his belief in the instantaneous character of entire sanctification on at least four grounds:

1. *It is done in response to faith.* Early in his experience, he believed that this stage of grace occurred only late in life after a lengthy process of maturation. However, he came to see that since it is by faith, there is no reason why one should not claim this "blessing" early on in one's spiritual pilgrimage. Of course, he always deferred to the sovereignty of God and did not believe one should feel any sense of guilt if God had not chosen to effect the great inward transformation.

2. *Experience.* After carefully examining the testimonies of numerous persons, he reached the conclusion that all had experienced the great transformation in an instant. True, this moment was both preceded and followed by gradual sanctification or growth in grace, but the actual deliverance from inward sin was instantaneous.

3. *Logic.* By drawing an analogy with the gradual approach of death, he demonstrated how there is a logical moment at which entire sanctification occurs. His own description of this reasoning is quite clear:

> A man may be dying for some time; yet he does not properly speaking, die, till the soul is separated from the body; and in that instant, he lives the life of eternity. In like manner, he may be dying to sin for some time; yet he is not dead to sin, till sin is separated from his soul; and in that instant, he lives the full life of love. And as the change undergone, when the body dies, is of a different kind, and infinitely greater than any we had known before, yea, such as till then, it is impossible to conceive; so the change wrought, when the soul dies to sin, is of a different kind, and infinitely greater than any before, and that any can conceive, till he experiences it. Yet he still grows in grace, in the knowledge of Christ, in the love and image of God; and will do so, not only till death, but through all eternity.[22]

Here again we see how Wesley emphasizes the correlation of process and moment, allowing neither to disappear from the experience of the believer. The instant of entire sanctification is a point in a lifelong process.

4. *The nature of sin.* As we have seen, Wesley understood the nature of sin to be self-will. This, he argued, is the root of all sin. All acts that are sinful are expressions of this "seed." One must be careful not to be confused by the metaphors, "root" and "seed," and think of them as referring to some "thing" within the person. It is the universal bent of fallen humanity toward self-sovereignty that remains, though it does not reign, in believers.

It is in the light of this understanding of sin that Wesley's words have meaning. Since they are so precise and clear, we simply quote them:

> although we may *weaken* our enemies day by day; yet we cannot *drive them out*. By all the grace which is given at justification we cannot extirpate them. Though we watch and pray ever so much, we cannot wholly cleanse either our hearts or hands. Most sure we cannot, till it shall please our Lord to speak to our hearts again, to speak the second time, "Be clean"; and then only the leprosy is cleansed. Then only, the evil root, the carnal mind, is destroyed; and inbred sin subsists no more.[23]

Wesley was able to maintain a proper balance between the process and the moment, something many of those who are his spiritual children have been unable to do. But if we are going to have a doctrine that is livable, both must be kept in view. I participated in a conference on church renewal in the Wesleyan holiness tradition. One of the papers was presented by General Superintendent Lee M. Haines of The Wesleyan Church, in which he said:

> *We must renew our vision of sanctification as both a pilgrimage and an event,* as a process and a relationship with a history, a healing and a healthy growth, a quest and a gift. We must not reduce sanctification to a single moment

in time. Neither must we forget the importance of such a moment of commitment on our part and the bringing of wholeness on God's part, allowing all of that to be eroded away in the partial truth of gradual development. It has been extremely difficult for the followers of Wesley to maintain his synthesis of the event and the process. The pendulum has swung widely from one extreme to another, and is still swinging at the present time. But if the renewal movement is to be renewed, we must honestly face the paradox of a moment and a lifetime, both of which are necessary if we are to be holy as he is holy.

If we diagram the Christian life, we run the risk of creating a stereotype such as we have spoken against. Yet, with its limitations, such a picture can give us some insight into a normal development of grace in human life.

The late Bishop Leslie R. Marston of the Free Methodist church spoke in a Wesleyan Theology Conference about the preaching he had heard while growing up in the church and referred to it as the "plateau concept." As I recall my early experience of holiness preaching, it generally reflected the same pattern. Bishop Marston diagramed it like this:

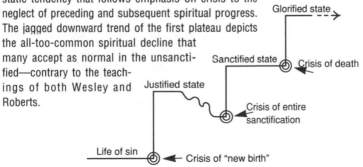

A. The "Plateau Concept" is a misrepresentation of normal Christian experience and growth, held neither by Wesley nor by Roberts. The diagram represents the static tendency that follows emphasis on crisis to the neglect of preceding and subsequent spiritual progress. The jagged downward trend of the first plateau depicts the all-too-common spiritual decline that many accept as normal in the unsanctified—contrary to the teachings of both Wesley and Roberts.

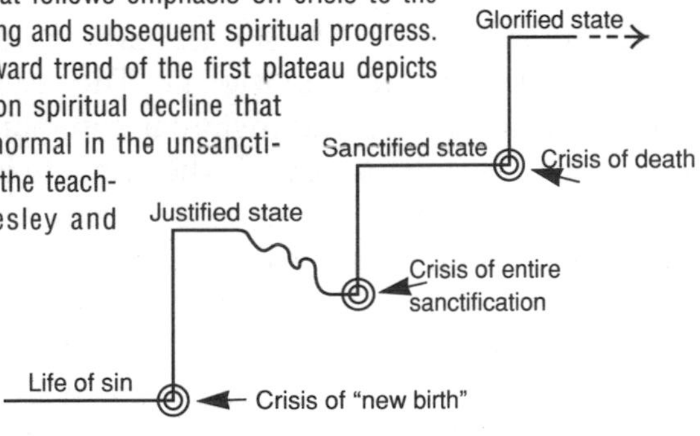

He then talked about the view of the Christian life that he had found presented in the writings of Benjamin T. Roberts (founder of the Free Methodist church). When I heard his presentation at the conference, I was very excited, because it was almost precisely the understanding I had derived from an intensive study of John Wesley's teaching, and I had used substantially the same diagram in my own teaching. Bishop Marston's representation looked like this:

B. The "Dynamic Concept" of Christian experience and growth prevails in the teachings of both Wesley and Roberts, emphasizing progress between crises. Roberts, however, conceived of Christian perfection as the normal progress of every fully obedient and believing Christian, whereas Wesley identified Christian perfection with entire sanctification.

NOTE: In both diagrams the coiled-spring symbol at points of crisis is intended to indicate that the direction of growth changes in consequence of an inner work of divine grace.

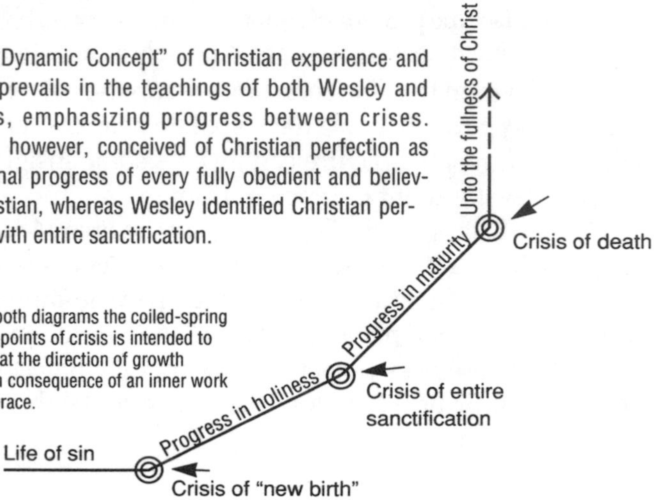

The above charts accompany and are a part of "The Crisis-Process Issue in Wesleyan Thought," a paper presented before the Wesleyan Theological Society at Olivet Nazarene College, November 2, 1968, by Leslie R. Marston.

This approach to the Christian life is far more exciting and truer to a biblical picture than the first. The beauty of it is that it integrates progressive and instantaneous sanctification in a fashion that is consistent with the way life is lived out.

The shape of the moment of experience we call entire sanctification is influenced by a number of factors: personality, environment, culture, socioeconomic status, and no doubt many others. For some persons, that moment is marked by a traumatic struggle with surrender to the will of God as they understand it. In their case it becomes a real crisis. For others, it is a gentle transition perhaps hardly noticeable at its passing because they are simply walking on in the sincere quest for the fullness of God. The difference in the character of the experience does not in any case invalidate its reality.

Dr. Daniel Steele, early scholar in the holiness movement and professor at Boston University, recognized this truth and gave wise counsel to the young minister who was leaving the classroom for the parish.

> We learn from books and from the lectures of some theological professors that both regeneration and entire sanctification are states of grace sharply defined, entered upon instantaneously after certain definite steps, and followed by certain very marked results. But the young preacher soon learns that there are eminently spiritual members of his church whose experiences have not been in accordance with this regulation manner. They have passed through no marked and memorable crises. Hence they have no spiritual anniversaries. The young pastor is puzzled by these anomalies. At last, if he is wise he will conclude that the books describe normal experiences to which the Holy Spirit does not limit itself, and that an abnormal method of gaining a spiritual change or elevation is by no means to be discounted.[24]

The American holiness movement emerged in the midst of a cultural situation that accentuated highly emotional religious experiences. Evangelism in this setting as it was practiced in the frontier camp meeting and the protracted meeting resulted in varied and unusual demonstrations such as "barking," passing into unconsciousness, and vocal praise to God. When holiness evangelists took over the methods of the revivalists, the same responses were generated as persons came to the "mourner's bench" to seek entire sanctification. These were all valid expressions of genuine religious experience. Many persons today still find fulfillment and meaning in this form of religious expression. But other personality types, and socio-cultural-economic development have led equally devout and religious people to experience sanctifying grace in less dramatic ways, though just as real and transforming. It seems important to recognize for oneself as well as others that God respects our individuality and does not squeeze us into a form of religious expression that violates and thus in a sense destroys our uniqueness.

Many sincere persons have left the holiness movement simply because strong personalities have attempted to foist their own type of experience upon others. When they could not conform to these types of experience, they sought an environment less oppressive. We should be mature enough to recognize that God allows each one of us to be ourselves within the context of the sanctifying work of the Holy Spirit.

How do we prepare to receive God's sanctifying grace? As we have said before, there are no magic formulas that lead automatically into the relation called entire sanctification. But there are some clues from Scripture and experience as to the kinds of things we must do.

In the Old Testament we noted how the ceremonial practices set persons or things apart for God's ownership or service. In fact, most emphasis is laid upon the human part, our sanctification of ourselves in this sense. No doubt this influences Paul's exhortation to those who have been justified, appealing to them to yield or present themselves to God. In Rom. 6:13 he says, "Offer yourselves to God, as those who have been brought from death to life; and offer the parts of your body to him as instruments of righteousness." This is reiterated in verse 19 when he exhorts, "Now offer [the parts of your body] in slavery to righteousness leading to holiness."

His point is that this is the logical thing to do. Now that one has been transported from being "in Adam" to being "in Christ" and become alive unto God, one should carry through the logical implications of that work of grace by this act of complete consecration. We may thus suggest that a full and complete consecration is one important element in appropriating the grace of entire sanctification.

John Wesley generally speaks about three aspects of one's purposeful pursuit of full salvation. The first of these is *repentance.* This is different from the first repentance that precedes and prepares for saving faith. It basically involves two matters: self-knowledge and awareness of one's inability to cleanse oneself from remaining sin.

This suggests that a sense of need is fundamental to receiving God's sanctifying grace. When one becomes conscious of this inward disposition to self-sovereignty that is referred to in the New Testament as carnal mindedness or "the flesh," the way is prepared to cry out to God for deliverance. Alongside of this consciousness is the equally important sense that our own strength is incapable of overcoming it or putting it to death.

Then comes *mortification,* meaning the putting away the marks of the old life and by means of spiritual exercises and discipline seeking to bring our lives into conformity to God's will. This seems to imply a gradual elimination of manifestations of self-centered behavior. The final step is *faith,* which is the appropriation of the promises of God. Faith answers to the second aspect of repentance and recognizes our complete dependence upon the work of the Spirit to cleanse away the remnants of sin (self-will) that are present in the born-again believer.

Alongside these special considerations, Wesley emphasized the practice of those regular Christian disciplines: prayer, Bible reading, worship, partaking of the sacraments and other means of grace. All these further the work of sanctification in human life, not only leading to the stage of perfect love but also enhancing the Christian life to its climax in glorification.

SPIRITUAL FORMATION EXERCISES

Clarifying the Concepts

A Content Quiz

1. Making a one size fits all formula of steps to entire sanctification is risky business because:
   A. of the danger of creating religious clones
   B. this trivializes the sovereignty of God
   C. such formulas fail to account for the cultural factors that often shape religious experiences
   D. the Bible itself does not specify invariable particular steps to sanctification
   E. all of the above
2. Sanctification:
   A. is a lifelong process
   B. is an instantaneous experience in which the believer is perfected in love
   C. occurs in that moment in which God delivers the believer from all inward sin
   D. begins at the new birth and continues until death—and beyond
   E. all of the above
3. John Wesley based his doctrine of instantaneous sanctification upon:
   A. the fact that sanctifying grace comes by faith
   B. observation of the experience of God's people
   C. logic
   D. the nature of sin
   E. all of the above
4. Which of the following is (are) used in chapter 8 to speak of crisis and process in our experience of sanctification?
   A. pilgrimage and event
   B. a quest and a gift
   C. progressive and instantaneous
   D. the paradox of a *moment* and a *lifetime*
   E. all of the above

5. While there are no magic formulas for receiving entire sanctification, some general directions are offered for the seeker in chapter 8 including which of the following?

A. complete consecration
B. awareness that one cannot cleanse his own heart
C. mortification
D. engaging in prayer, Bible study, worship, and partaking of the sacrament of holy Communion
E. all of the above

(The answer to each of the five preceding quiz questions is *all of the above.*)

Exploring Feelings and Attitudes

Many persons who were willing to do whatever it took to find full salvation discovered that there was no shortage of people who were willing to tell them just what to do. Usually, however, the counsel was based on the adviser's own experience of grace. "If I saw men as trees walking, then you should too," was the common belief. But when someone else's experience did not fit them, many believers suffered, struggled, made premature professions, and finally gave up in despair. Some even succumbed to a creeping cynicism or became just plain bitter.

If any of the preceding conditions match your experience, find a place of prayer and offer to God all the past pain, disappointment, or bitterness. Write down the negative feelings that have been building up and offer them up to God. Then, in the sunshine of His blessing walk away from those past negative experiences in the quiet confidence that the God who made you knows how to reach you when it comes to spiritual experience.

Application to Life

What I learned or reviewed about the variety of religious experiences, the sovereignty of God, the nature of faith, and the ways in which culture can shape the way we express spirituality tells me that I should:

A. be slow to judge the spirituality of others
B. wait patiently for the Lord to deal with me in His own way
C. be tolerant of those whose experience of religion differs from mine
D. rest in the assurance that if I faithfully follow Jesus in devotion and service while seeking sanctifying grace that God will send it when He has adequately prepared my heart for it
E. all of the above

9

Sanctification and Final Salvation

The subject with which we propose to conclude this brief discussion is a very delicate one and presents us with several pitfalls. But it is a most important topic if we would maintain sound doctrine. Careful distinctions are necessary in order to avoid perverting the truth. Tradition is also very strong, and many people have deep-rooted opinions. Nothing can disturb the waters like calling such prejudices into question.

First we need to define what we mean by "final salvation." Usually, that conjures up pictures of heaven in people's minds, but quite interestingly, the New Testament says very little about heaven as the final abode of the righteous. Most simply, when we refer to final salvation we are referring to final acceptance by God. We may then put the question this way: Does God require something different or more for final acceptance than He does to accept us into His favor initially?

No theological position in the history of classical Christian theology has answered this question affirmatively. That is, all have affirmed that the basis of initial acceptance with God is the same basis on which He accepts us into His eternal presence.

This brings us back to our earlier discussion of the relation between justification and sanctification. As we saw there, the medieval Catholic tradition took the position that one had to become fully holy prior to justification. This means that entire sanctification is the basis of entrance into the favor of God and ultimately "into heaven." But since only a select few, they thought, ever achieved this status in this life, purgatory became a necessity as a place where the process of sanctification could be completed.

The Protestant Reformation insisted that God accepts us now and finally on the basis of a "righteousness" not our own. Martin Luther taught that we can never be holy in this life. In fact he insisted on it, even encouraging his followers to "sin boldly." But he still held to the position that ethical righteousness was necessary to acceptance with God both now and at the end. This is how he came up with the view of "imputed righteousness"– a righteousness of Another as the basis of final salvation.

We saw in our earlier discussion, however, that the Bible teaches that we are accepted by God on the basis of faith. By faith we are accounted righteous, not ethically but in the sense of being in right relation to God. And this becomes the basis of our final acceptance with God as well. As J. Kenneth Grider puts it, "Eternal destiny is settled at the first work of grace."

If ethical righteousness is the basis of final salvation, we must ask, Who then can be saved? Honesty requires us to recognize that there is no such state of grace in this life as sinless perfection. This is why we have argued in this essay that purity of heart is purity of intention, not perfect performance. Faith in the mercy of God can be the only possible basis of our confidence. As Mr. Wesley lay dying, he said, "I the chief of sinners am, but Jesus died for me." This is the ultimate plea for all of us.

But what about the holy life? Where does sanctification fit into all this? That is where we face the need for very careful distinctions that will require our close attention.

We must first establish an important doctrinal point. Unlike the Calvinist, the Wesleyan believes that while the ability to do so is God-given, each person must choose to respond to the gospel. Grace is not irresistible. For the same reasons, the Wesleyan rejects the idea of "once in grace, always in grace." This means that one's continued relation to God depends on a walk of obedience.

It is very critical to understand that this walk of obedience does not become a basis for acceptance with God. That acceptance is always based on faith in God's love and mercy. But this faith, if it is genuine, will manifest itself as authentic by the pursuit of holiness of heart and life.

Since our relation to God is conditional in nature, one may forfeit that relation by disobedience or neglect. The Bible clearly teaches this principle. Therefore it may be stated that the *pursuit* of holiness is a condition of final salvation (see Heb. 12:14).

Nonetheless, this does not say that a certain degree of holiness must be reached or even given by God. For this reason Wesley wisely insisted that entire sanctification must be preached in a drawing rather than a driving manner.[25]

In response to the question, "Does not the harshly preaching perfection tend to bring believers into a kind of bondage, or slavish fear?" he answered, "It does: Therefore we should always place it in the most amiable light, so that it may excite only hope, joy, and desire."[26]

Neither should the fact that we have not experienced full salvation be the occasion for fear of dying before this great deliverance. It should be a matter of concern and earnest seeking but not tormenting fear. What is important is the pursuit in the confidence of full acceptance with God and the hope in the promises of God for complete cleansing.

In the Wesleyan understanding, continuing in faith is the fundamental and ultimate condition of final salvation. This walk of faith will result sooner or later in perfect sanctification. After all, God is faithful to His word, and we live by

His promises. In this way we walk a narrow path that avoids antinomianism (disregard for the law that sees no necessity for holy living) on the one hand and works-righteousness on the other. It takes seriously both our confidence in faith alone as the basis of salvation and our accountability to God to pursue the holy way.

SPIRITUAL FORMATION EXERCISES

Clarifying the Concepts

Worth Remembering

This chapter is loaded with powerful ideas that are "worth remembering." Find the context of the following excerpts, paraphrases, and ideas in the chapter and think about their significance.

1. Final acceptance with God or eternal destiny is settled at the first work of grace.
2. Purity of heart is purity of intention.
3. Each person must choose to respond to the gospel—grace is not irresistible.
4. The obedience of the sanctified does not ever become the basis for acceptance with God.
5. Pursuit of holiness may be the condition of final acceptance with God.
6. Entire sanctification must be preached in a *drawing* rather than a *driving* manner.
7. The fact that a sincere believer has not yet been fully sanctified should not produce tormenting fear that he may die before deliverance comes.
8. Faith is the fundamental and ultimate condition of final salvation.

Exploring Feelings and Attitudes

Select one or two of the preceding "worth remembering"

statements. Tonight, instead of watching television, spend at least one hour in thought, meditation, prayer, and relaxation with this chosen theme. Relaxation? Yes, spiritual relaxation in the company of a noble thought and in the presence of God is not a waste of time.

Application to Life

Look at the opportunities for Christian service that loom before you. In the near future are you going to make a speech, lead family worship, participate in a small-group meeting, give a testimony in the midweek service, teach a Sunday School class, write a letter, or have coffee with a friend in need of spiritual guidance?

From the "worth remembering" list find some ideas that you can use in one or more Christian service opportunities you have this week. Why not share something "worth remembering" today?

Epilogue

The clearest statement of a doctrine of Christian experience is worthless unless accompanied by a hunger for the reality. The tragedy of history is that most religious movements that began with an all-consuming passion for "the simplicity and spiritual power of the primitive New Testament church" eventually became organizations preoccupied with their own existence. The initial impulse faded, and the ideals of the fathers became crystallized into dogma without life.

It is my earnest desire that the reader of this essay will find understanding of some of the major issues that surround the doctrine of sanctification. But I have a more burning desire that the reader will know the "hungering and thirsting after righteousness" that will pursue the ideal, will experience that "homesickness for holiness" that has marked sincere souls throughout Christian history.

If one analyzes the Wesley hymns, he will sense the desire for fullness that no doubt was the life breath of that movement in its prime. The aspiration for holiness comes to poetic expression in many ways. Let's close with a few verses from one of these hymns of aspiration, accompanied by a heartfelt prayer that they may become *our* prayer.

Love divine, all loves excelling,
Joy of heav'n, to earth come down!
Fix in us Thy humble dwelling;
All Thy faithful mercies crown.
Jesus, Thou art all compassion;
Pure, unbounded love Thou art.
Visit us with Thy salvation;
Enter ev'ry trembling heart.

Finish then Thy new creation;
Pure and spotless let us be.
Let us see Thy great salvation,
Perfectly restored in Thee:
Changed from glory into glory,
Till in heav'n we take our place,
Till we cast our crowns before Thee,
Lost in wonder, love, and praise.

—CHARLES WESLEY

Endnotes

1. W. T. Purkiser, *Interpreting Christian Holiness* (Kansas City: Beacon Hill Press of Kansas City, 1971), 9.

2. See Frank G. Carver, "Biblical Foundations for the 'Secondness' of Entire Sanctification," *Wesleyan Theological Journal.* Vol. 22, No. 2; Fall 1987, 7-23.

3. Gordon J. Wenham, *The Book of Leviticus* (Grand Rapids: William B. Eerdmans Publishing Co., 1979), 22.

4. David Hill, *Greek Words and Hebrew Meanings* (Cambridge: Cambridge University Press, 1967), 232-33.

5. John Wesley, *The Standard Sermons of John Wesley,* 2 vols., ed. E. H. Sugden (London: Epworth Press, 1961), 2:225.

6. E. Stanley Jones, *The Way to Power and Poise* (New York: Abingdon-Cokesbury Press, 1949), 42.

7. James S. Stewart, *A Man in Christ* (New York: Harper and Row, Publishers, n.d.), 308.

8. Gerhard von Rad, *Genesis, a Bible Commentary for Teaching and Preaching* (Philadelphia: Westminster Press, 1972), 198-99.

9. A full scholarly treatment of this topic can be found in Mildred Bangs Wynkoop, *A Theology of Love* (Kansas City: Beacon Hill Press of Kansas City, 1972).

10. John Wesley, *Works of John Wesley,* 3rd ed., 14 vols. (London: Wesleyan Methodist Book Room, 1872; reprint, Kansas City: Beacon Hill Press of Kansas City, 1978), 5:244 f.

11. *Works* 6:488.

12. John Wesley, *A Plain Account of Christian Perfection* (Kansas City: Beacon Hill Press of Kansas City, 1968), 55.

13. *Standard Sermons* 2:80.

14. John Wesley, *Letters of the Reverend John Wesley,* ed. John Telford (London: Epworth Press, 1931), 1:76.

15. *Works* 8:341.

16. *Works* 10:68; 6:71.

17. John Wesley, *Explanatory Notes upon the New Testament* (London: Epworth Press, 1954), note on Eph. 5:28.

18. *Standard Sermons* 2:253.

19. Ibid., 2:324 f.

20. Wynkoop, *Theology of Love,* 158.

21. It is easy to find apparent exceptions to this principle. Theologically, we attribute this "unconverted goodness" to prevenient grace, not natural goodness or the absence of sin in some persons. To say that would contradict the clear teaching of Scripture.

22. *Plain Account of Christian Perfection,* 62.

23. *Standard Sermons* 2:390 f.

24. Daniel Steele, *Steele's Answers* (Chicago: Christian Witness Co., 1912), 128.

25. *Works* 8:286.

26. Ibid., 297.

Bibliography

Recommended for Further Reading

Cook, Thomas. *New Testament Holiness.* London: Epworth Press, 1950.

Cox, Leo. *John Wesley's Concept of Perfection.* Kansas City: Beacon Hill Press, 1964.

Exploring Christian Holiness, 3 vols. Kansas City: Beacon Hill Press of Kansas City, 1985.

Great Holiness Classics, 5 vols. Kansas City: Beacon Hill Press of Kansas City, various dates.

Greathouse, W. M., and Dunning, H. Ray. *Introduction to Wesleyan Theology,* revised. Kansas City: Beacon Hill Press of Kansas City, 1989.

Lindstrom, Harald. *Wesley and Sanctification.* Asbury, Ky.: Francis Asbury Publishing Co., n.d.

Wesley, John. *A Plain Account of Christian Perfection.* Kansas City: Beacon Hill Press of Kansas City, 1968.

Wynkoop, Mildred Bangs. *A Theology of Love.* Kansas City: Beacon Hill Press of Kansas City, 1972.